D0519152

19

THE NEW TEMPLE SHAKESPEARE

Edited by M. R. Ridley, M.A.

THE
COMEDY OF ERRORS

by William Shakespeare

100126
822

London: J. M. DENT & SONS LTD.
New York: E. P. DUTTON & CO. INC.

This book is copyright. It may not be reproduced in part or in whole by any method without written permission. Application should be made to the publishers:

J. M. DENT & SONS LTD.
Aldine House · Bedford St. · London

Made in Great Britain
by
The Temple Press · Letchworth · Herts

First published . . 1934
Last reprinted . . 1948

PRINTED IN GREAT BRITAIN BY
MORRISON AND GIBB LTD., LONDON AND EDINBURGH

SOMERSET
COUNTY
LIBRARY

Editor's General Note

The Text. The editor has kept before him the aim of presenting to the modern reader the nearest possible approximation to what Shakespeare actually wrote. The text is therefore conservative, and is based on the earliest reliable printed text. But to avoid distraction (*a*) the spelling is modernised, and (*b*) a limited number of universally accepted emendations is admitted without comment. Where a Quarto text exists as well as the First Folio the passages which occur only in the Quarto are enclosed in square brackets [ ] and those which occur only in the Folio in brace brackets { }.

Scene Division. The rapid continuity of the Elizabethan curtainless production is lost by the 'traditional' scene divisions. Where there is an essential difference of place these scene divisions are retained. Where on the other hand the change of place is insignificant the scene division is indicated only by a space on the page. For ease of reference, however, the 'traditional' division is retained at the head of the page and in line numbering.

Notes. Passages on which there are notes are indicated by a † in the margin.

Punctuation adheres more closely than has been usual to the 'Elizabethan' punctuation of the early texts. It is often therefore more indicative of the way in which the lines were to be delivered than of their syntactical construction.

Glossaries are arranged on a somewhat novel principle, not alphabetically, but in the order in which the words or phrases occur. The editor is much indebted to Mr J. N. Bryson for his collaboration in the preparation of the glossaries.

Preface

The Text.   The only text of this play is that of the First Folio. It was very probably, judging by a number of apparently auditory errors and the unusual normality of the spelling, set from a copy of the original which had been taken down from dictation.   There are comparatively few corrupt or difficult passages.

Date of Composition.   There is direct evidence, in the shape of an account of the Christmas revels at Gray's Inn in 1594-5, that the play is earlier than 1594.   General stylistic tests, together with one or two somewhat slender pieces of internal evidence, point to the generally accepted date, 1590-1.

Source.   This is plain sailing.   The play is a straight adaptation of the *Menæchmi* of Plautus, with one scene (III. i.) lifted from the *Amphitryo*.   It is possible that Shakespeare had seen in manuscript a translation of the *Menæchmi* which appeared in 1595. The New Cambridge editors favour the view that Shakespeare was working from an older play, based on the *Menæchmi*, and that this play was *The Historie of Error*, which was performed at Hampton Court as far back as 1576-7.

Duration of Action.   The play conforms strictly to the ' unity of time ' and reasonably strictly to the ' unity of place.'

Criticism.   The play is thoroughly competent and ' slick ' 'prentice work, going one (or indeed two) better than its model in the complications of the old time-worn mistaken-identity motive ; and apart from a few stray passages might, one feels, ' have been written by anyone.'

THE COMEDY OF ERRORS

DRAMATIS PERSONÆ

SOLINUS, *duke of Ephesus.*
ÆGEON, *a merchant of Syracuse.*
ANTIPHOLUS of Ephesus, ⎫ *twin brothers and sons to*
ANTIPHOLUS of Syracuse,⎭ *Ægeon and Æmilia.*
DROMIO of Ephesus, ⎫ *twin brothers, and attendants*
DROMIO of Syracuse, ⎭ *on the two Antipholuses.*
BALTHAZAR, *a merchant.*
ANGELO, *a goldsmith.*
First Merchant, *friend to Antipholus of Syracuse.*
Second Merchant, *to whom Angelo is a debtor.*
PINCH, *a schoolmaster.*

ÆMILIA, *wife to Ægeon, an Abbess at Ephesus.*
ADRIANA, *wife to Antipholus of Ephesus.*
LUCIANA, *her sister.*
LUCE, *servant to Adriana.*
A Courtezan.

Gaoler, Officers, and other Attendants.

SCENE: *Ephesus.*

THE COMEDY OF ERRORS

Act First

SCENE I

A hall in the Duke's palace

Enter Duke Solinus, Ægeon, Gaoler, Officers, and other Attendants

Æg. Proceed, Solinus, to procure my fall,
And by the doom of death end woes and all.

Du. Merchant of Syracusa, plead no more ;
I am not partial to infringe our laws :
The enmity and discord which of late
Sprung from the rancorous outrage of your duke
To merchants, our well-dealing countrymen,
Who, wanting guilders to redeem their lives,
Have seal'd his rigorous statutes with their bloods,
Excludes all pity from our threatening looks.   10
For, since the mortal and intestine jars
'Twixt thy seditious countrymen and us,
It hath in solemn synods been decreed,
Both by the Syracusians and ourselves,

I

To admit no traffic to our adverse towns :
Nay more, if any born at Ephesus
Be seen at Syracusian marts and fairs ;
Again, if any Syracusian born
Come to the bay of Ephesus, he dies ;
His goods confiscate to the duke's dispose,   **20**
Unless a thousand marks be levied,
To quit the penalty and to ransom him.
Thy substance, valued at the highest rate,
Cannot amount unto a hundred marks,
Therefore by law thou art condemn'd to die.

Æg. Yet this my comfort, when your words are done,
My woes end likewise with the evening sun.

Du. Well, Syracusian, say, in brief, the cause
Why thou departed'st from thy native home,
And for what cause thou cam'st to Ephesus.   **30**

Æg. A heavier task could not have been impos'd
Than I to speak my griefs unspeakable :
Yet that the world may witness that my end
Was wrought by nature, not by vile offence,
I'll utter what my sorrow gives me leave.
In Syracusa was I born, and wed
Unto a woman, happy but for me,
And by me ; had not our hap been bad :
With her I liv'd in joy, our wealth increas'd

2

By prosperous voyages I often made   40
To Epidamnum, till my factor's death,
And the great care of goods at random left,
Drew me from kind embracements of my spouse :
From whom my absence was not six months old,
Before herself (almost at fainting under
The pleasing punishment that women bear)
Had made provision for her following me,
And soon and safe arrived where I was :
There had she not been long, but she became
A joyful mother of two goodly sons ;   50
And, which was strange, the one so like the other
As could not be distinguish'd but by names.
That very hour, and in the self-same inn,
A meaner woman was delivered
Of such a burthen male, twins both alike :
Those, for their parents were exceeding poor,
I bought, and brought up to attend my sons.
My wife, not meanly proud of two such boys,
Made daily motions for our home return :
Unwilling I agreed ; alas ! too soon   60
We came aboard.
A league from Epidamnum had we sail'd,
Before the always wind-obeying deep
Gave any tragic instance of our harm :

3

But longer did we not retain much hope;
For what obscured light the heavens did grant
Did but convey unto our fearful minds
A doubtful warrant of immediate death,
Which though myself would gladly have embrac'd,
Yet the incessant weepings of my wife,   70
Weeping before for what she saw must come,
And piteous plainings of the pretty babes,
That mourn'd for fashion, ignorant what to fear,
Forc'd me to seek delays for them and me.
And this it was: (for other means was none)
The sailors sought for safety by our boat,
And left the ship, then sinking-ripe, to us:
My wife, more careful for the latter-born,
Had fasten'd him unto a small spare mast,
Such as seafaring men provide for storms;   80
To him one of the other twins was bound,
Whilst I had been like heedful of the other:
The children thus dispos'd, my wife and I,
Fixing our eyes on whom our care was fix'd,
Fasten'd ourselves at either end the mast,
And floating straight, obedient to the stream,
Was carried towards Corinth, as we thought.
At length the sun, gazing upon the earth,
Dispers'd those vapours that offended us,

4

And, by the benefit of his wished light,   90
The seas wax'd calm, and we discovered
Two ships from far, making amain to us ;
Of Corinth that, of Epidaurus this :
But ere they came,—O, let me say no more !
Gather the sequel by that went before.

Du. Nay, forward, old man, do not break off so,
For we may pity, though not pardon thee.

Æg. O, had the gods done so, I had not now
Worthily term'd them merciless to us :
For, ere the ships could meet by twice five leagues,   100
We were encounter'd by a mighty rock,
Which being violently borne upon,
Our helpful ship was splitted in the midst ;
So that, in this unjust divorce of us,
Fortune had left to both of us alike
What to delight in, what to sorrow for.
Her part, poor soul, seeming as burdened
With lesser weight, but not with lesser woe,
Was carried with more speed before the wind,
And in our sight they three were taken up   110
By fishermen of Corinth, as we thought.
At length, another ship had seiz'd on us,
And, knowing whom it was their hap to save,
Gave healthful welcome to their shipwreck'd guests,

And would have reft the fishers of their prey,
Had not their bark been very slow of sail;
And therefore homeward did they bend their
    course.
Thus have you heard me sever'd from my bliss,
That by misfortunes was my life prolong'd,
To tell sad stories of my own mishaps.   120

Du. And for the sake of them thou sorrowest for,
Do me the favour to dilate at full
What hath befall'n of them and thee till now.

Æg. My youngest boy, and yet my eldest care,
At eighteen years became inquisitive
After his brother; and importun'd me
That his attendant—so his case was like,
Reft of his brother, but retain'd his name—
Might bear him company in the quest of him:
Whom whilst I labour'd of a love to see,   130
I hazarded the loss of whom I lov'd.
Five summers have I spent in farthest Greece,
Roaming clean through the bounds of Asia,
And, coasting homeward, came to Ephesus;
Hopeless to find, yet loath to leave unsought
Or that, or any place that harbours men.
But here must end the story of my life,
And happy were I in my timely death,

Could all my travels warrant me they live.

Du. Hapless Ægeon, whom the fates have mark'd   140
To bear the extremity of dire mishap:
Now, trust me, were it not against our laws,
Against my crown, my oath, my dignity,
Which princes, would they, may not disannul,
My soul should sue as advocate for thee:
But, though thou art adjudged to the death,
And passed sentence may not be recall'd
But to our honour's great disparagement;
Yet will I favour thee in what I can:
Therefore, merchant, I'll limit thee this day   150
To seek thy help by beneficial help:
Try all the friends thou hast in Ephesus,
Beg thou, or borrow, to make up the sum,
And live; if no, then thou art doom'd to die.
Gaoler, take him to thy custody.

Gaol. I will, my lord.

Æg. Hopeless and helpless doth Ægeon wend,
But to procrastinate his lifeless end.   *Exeunt*

°b   7

SCENE II

The Mart

*Enter Antipholus of Syracuse, Dromio of Syracuse, and
First Merchant*

1.M. Therefore give out you are of Epidamnum,
    Lest that your goods too soon be confiscate:
    This very day a Syracusian merchant
    Is apprehended for arrival here,
    And not being able to buy out his life,
    According to the statute of the town,
    Dies ere the weary sun set in the west:
    There is your money that I had to keep.

A.S. Go bear it to the Centaur, where we host,
    And stay there, Dromio, till I come to thee;   **10**
    Within this hour it will be dinner-time:
    Till that, I'll view the manners of the town,
    Peruse the traders, gaze upon the buildings,
    And then return and sleep within mine inn,
    For with long travel I am stiff and weary.
    Get thee away.

D.S. Many a man would take you at your word,
    And go indeed, having so good a mean.   *Exit*

A.S. A trusty villain, sir, that very oft,

8

When I am dull with care and melancholy,   20
Lightens my humour with his merry jests :
What, will you walk with me about the town,
And then go to my inn and dine with me ?

1.M. I am invited, sir, to certain merchants,
Of whom I hope to make much benefit ;
I crave your pardon ; soon at five o'clock,
Please you, I 'll meet with you upon the mart,
And afterward consort you till bed-time :
My present business calls me from you now.

A.S. Farewell till then : I will go lose myself,   30
And wander up and down to view the city.

1.M. Sir, I commend you to your own content.   *Exit*

A.S. He that commends me to mine own content
Commends me to the thing I cannot get :
I to the world am like a drop of water,
That in the ocean seeks another drop,
Who, falling there to find his fellow forth,
Unseen, inquisitive, confounds himself :
So I, to find a mother and a brother,
In quest of them, unhappier, lose myself.   40

Enter Dromio of Ephesus

Here comes the almanac of my true date :
What now ? how chance thou art return'd so soon ?

D.E. Return'd so soon ! rather approach'd too late :

9

    The capon burns, the pig falls from the spit;
    The clock hath strucken twelve upon the bell;
    My mistress made it one upon my cheek:
    She is so hot, because the meat is cold;
    The meat is cold, because you come not home;
    You come not home, because you have no stomach;
    You have no stomach, having broke your fast;   50
    But we, that know what 'tis to fast and pray,
    Are penitent for your default to-day.

*A.S.*Stop in your wind, sir: tell me this, I pray:
    Where have you left the money that I gave you?

*D.E.*O,—sixpence, that I had o' Wednesday last,
    To pay the saddler for my mistress' crupper?
    The saddler had it, sir, I kept it not.

*A.S.*I am not in a sportive humour now:
    Tell me, and dally not, where is the money?
    We being strangers here, how dar'st thou trust   60
    So great a charge from thine own custody?

*D.E.*I pray you, jest, sir, as you sit at dinner:
    I from my mistress come to you in post;
    If I return, I shall be post indeed,
    For she will score your fault upon my pate.
    Methinks your maw, like mine, should be your clock,
    And strike you home without a messenger.

*A.S.*Come, Dromio, come, these jests are out of season,

Reserve them till a merrier hour than this.
Where is the gold I gave in charge to thee ?   70

*D.E.*To me, sir ? why, you gave no gold to me.

*A.S.*Come on, sir knave, have done your foolishness,
And tell me how thou hast dispos'd thy charge.

*D.E.*My charge was but to fetch you from the mart
Home to your house, the Phœnix, sir, to dinner :
My mistress and her sister stays for you.

*A.S.*Now, as I am a Christian, answer me,
In what safe place you have bestow'd my money ;
Or I shall break that merry sconce of yours,
That stands on tricks when I am undispos'd :   80
Where is the thousand marks thou had'st of me ?

*D.E.*I have some marks of yours upon my pate ;
Some of my mistress' marks upon my shoulders ;
But not a thousand marks between you both.
If I should pay your worship those again,
Perchance you will not bear them patiently.

*A.S.*Thy mistress' marks ? what mistress, slave, hast thou ?

*D.E.*Your worship's wife, my mistress at the Phœnix ;
She that doth fast till you come home to dinner,
And prays that you will hie you home to dinner.   90

*A.S.*What, wilt thou flout me thus unto my face,
Being forbid ?   There, take you that, sir knave.

                                                Beats him

11

D.E. What mean you, sir ? for God's sake, hold your hands !
  Nay, an you will not, sir, I 'll take my heels.   *Exit*
A.S. Upon my life, by some device or other
  The villain is o'er-raught of all my money.
  They say this town is full of cozenage ;
  As, nimble jugglers that deceive the eye ;
  Dark-working sorcerers that change the mind ;
  Soul-killing witches that deform the body ;   100
  Disguised cheaters, prating mountebanks ;
  And many such-like liberties of sin :
  If it prove so, I will be gone the sooner.
  I 'll to the Centaur, to go seek this slave,
  I greatly fear my money is not safe.   *Exit*

Act Second

SCENE I

The house of Antipholus of Ephesus

Enter Adriana and Luciana

Adr. Neither my husband nor the slave return'd,
  That in such haste I sent to seek his master ?
  Sure, Luciana, it is two o'clock.
Luc. Perhaps some merchant hath invited him,

And from the mart he 's somewhere gone to dinner :
Good sister, let us dine, and never fret :
A man is master of his liberty :
Time is their master, and when they see time,
They 'll go or come : if so, be patient, sister.

Adr. Why should their liberty than ours be more ?   10
Luc. Because their business still lies out o' door.
Adr. Look, when I serve him so, he takes it ill.
Luc. O, know he is the bridle of your will.
Adr. There 's none but asses will be bridled so.
Luc. Why, headstrong liberty is lash'd with woe.
There 's nothing situate under heaven's eye
But hath his bound, in earth, in sea, in sky :
The beasts, the fishes, and the winged fowls,
Are their males' subjects, and at their controls :
Man more divine, the master of all these,   20
Lord of the wide world and wild watery seas,
Indued with intellectual sense and souls,
Of more pre-eminence than fish and fowls,
Are masters to their females, and their lords :
Then let your will attend on their accords.

Adr. This servitude makes you to keep unwed.
Luc. Not this, but troubles of the marriage-bed.
Adr. But, were you wedded, you would bear some sway.
Luc. Ere I learn love, I 'll practise to obey.

13

Adr. How if your husband start some other where ?   30

Luc. Till he come home again, I would forbear.

Adr. Patience unmov'd ! no marvel though she pause ;
     They can be meek that have no other cause :
     A wretched soul, bruis'd with adversity,
     We bid be quiet when we hear it cry ;
     But were we burden'd with like weight of pain,
     As much, or more, we should ourselves complain :
     So thou, that hast no unkind mate to grieve thee,
     With urging helpless patience wouldst relieve me ;
     But, if thou live to see like right bereft,   40
     This fool-begg'd patience in thee will be left.

Luc. Well, I will marry one day, but to try.
     Here comes your man ; now is your husband nigh.

                    Enter Dromio of Ephesus

Adr. Say, is your tardy master now at hand ?

D.E. Nay, he 's at two hands with me, and that my two ears
     can witness.

Adr. Say, didst thou speak with him ? know'st thou his
       mind ?

D.E. Ay, ay, he told his mind upon mine ear :
     Beshrew his hand, I scarce could understand it.

Luc. Spake he so doubtfully, thou couldst not feel his   50
     meaning ?

D.E. Nay, he struck so plainly, I could too well feel his

                            14

    blows ; and withal so doubtfully, that I could scarce
    understand them.

Adr. But say, I prithee, is he coming home ?

    It seems he hath great care to please his wife.

D.E. Why, mistress, sure my master is horn-mad.

Adr. Horn-mad, thou villain !

D.E.   I mean not cuckold-mad ;

    But, sure, he is stark mad.

    When I desir'd him to come home to dinner,   **60**

    He ask'd me for a thousand marks in gold :

    ' 'Tis dinner-time,' quoth I ; ' My gold ! ' quoth he ;

    ' Your meat doth burn,' quoth I ; ' My gold !' quoth he:

    ' Will you come home ? ' quoth I ; ' My gold !'
        quoth he,

    ' Where is the thousand marks I gave thee, villain ? '

    ' The pig,' quoth I, ' is burn'd ;' ' My gold !' quoth he:

    ' My mistress, sir,' quoth I ; ' Hang up thy mistress !

    I know not thy mistress ; out on thy mistress !'

Luc. Quoth who ?

D.E. Quoth my master :   **70**

    ' I know,' quoth he, ' no house, no wife, no mistress.'

    So that my errand, due unto my tongue,

    I thank him, I bare home upon my shoulders ;

    For, in conclusion, he did beat me there.

Adr. Go back again, thou slave, and fetch him home.

*D.E.*Go back again, and be new beaten home ?
     For God's sake, send some other messenger.
*Adr.*Back, slave, or I will break thy pate across.
*D.E.*And he will bless that cross with other beating :
     Between you, I shall have a holy head.   80
*Adr.*Hence, prating peasant ! fetch thy master home.
*D.E.*Am I so round with you, as you with me,
     That like a football you do spurn me thus ?
     You spurn me hence, and he will spurn me hither :
     If I last in this service, you must case me in leather.

                                                    Exit

Luc. Fie, how impatience loureth in your face !
*Adr.*His company must do his minions grace,
     Whilst I at home starve for a merry look.
     Hath homely age the alluring beauty took
     From my poor cheek ? then he hath wasted it :   90
     Are my discourses dull ? barren my wit ?
     If voluble and sharp discourse be marr'd,
     Unkindness blunts it more than marble hard :
     Do their gay vestments his affections bait ?
     That's not my fault ; he's master of my state :
     What ruins are in me that can be found,
     By him not ruin'd ? then is he the ground
     Of my defeatures.   My decayed fair
     A sunny look of his would soon repair :

                         16

But, too unruly deer, he breaks the pale,   100
    And feeds from home ; poor I am but his stale.
Luc. Self-harming jealousy ! fie, beat it hence !
Adr. Unfeeling fools can with such wrongs dispense :
    I know his eye doth homage otherwhere,
    Or else what lets it but he would be here ?
    Sister, you know he promis'd me a chain ;
    Would that alone o' love he would detain,
    So he would keep fair quarter with his bed !
    I see the jewel best enamelled
    Will lose his beauty ; yet the gold bides still,   110
    That others touch, and often touching will
    Where gold, and no man that hath a name,   †
    By falsehood and corruption doth it shame.
    Since that my beauty cannot please his eye,
    I 'll weep what 's left away, and weeping die.
Luc. How many fond fools serve mad jealousy !   *Exeunt*

SCENE II

A public place

Enter Antipholus of Syracuse

A.S. The gold I gave to Dromio is laid up
    Safe at the Centaur, and the heedful slave

17

Is wander'd forth in care to seek me out
By computation and mine host's report.
I could not speak with Dromio since at first
I sent him from the mart.   See, here he comes.

Enter Dromio of Syracuse

How now, sir? is your merry humour alter'd?
As you love strokes, so jest with me again.
You know no Centaur? you receiv'd no gold?
Your mistress sent to have me home to dinner?   10
My house was at the Phœnix?   Wast thou mad,
That thus so madly thou didst answer me?

D.S. What answer, sir? when spake I such a word?

A.S. Even now, even here, not half an hour since.

D.S. I did not see you since you sent me hence,
Home to the Centaur, with the gold you gave me.

A.S. Villain, thou didst deny the gold's receipt,
And told'st me of a mistress, and a dinner,
For which I hope thou felt'st I was displeas'd.

D.S. I am glad to see you in this merry vein: 20
What means this jest? I pray you, master, tell me.

A.S. Yea, dost thou jeer and flout me in the teeth?
Think'st thou I jest?   Hold, take thou that, and
          that.   *Beating him*

D.S. Hold, sir, for God's sake! now your jest is earnest:
Upon what bargain do you give it me?

A.S. Because that I familiarly sometimes
　　　Do use you for my fool, and chat with you,
　　　Your sauciness will jest upon my love,
　　　And make a common of my serious hours.
　　　When the sun shines, let foolish gnats make sport,　30
　　　But creep in crannies, when he hides his beams.
　　　If you will jest with me, know my aspect,
　　　And fashion your demeanour to my looks,
　　　Or I will beat this method in your sconce.

D.S. Sconce call you it ? so you would leave battering, I
　　　had rather have it a head : an you use these blows
　　　long, I must get a sconce for my head, and insconce it
　　　too, or else I shall seek my wit in my shoulders ; but,
　　　I pray, sir, why am I beaten ?

A.S. Dost thou not know ?　　　　　　　　　　　　40

D.S. Nothing, sir, but that I am beaten.

A.S. Shall I tell you why ?

D.S. Ay, sir, and wherefore ; for they say, every why hath
　　　a wherefore.

A.S. Why, first for flouting me, and then, wherefore,—
　　　For urging it the second time to me.

D.S. Was there ever any man thus beaten out of season,
　　　When in the why and the wherefore is neither rhyme
　　　　　　nor reason ?
　　　Well, sir, I thank you.

A.S. Thank me, sir, for what ? 50

D.S. Marry, sir, for this something that you gave me for nothing.

A.S. I 'll make you amends next, to give you nothing for something.   But say, sir, is it dinner-time ?

D.S. No sir, I think the meat wants that I have.

A.S. In good time, sir ; what 's that ?

D.S. Basting.

A.S. Well, sir, then 'twill be dry.

D.S. If it be, sir, I pray you, eat none of it.

A.S. Your reason ? 60

D.S. Lest it make you choleric, and purchase me another dry basting.

A.S. Well, sir, learn to jest in good time ; there 's a time for all things.

D.S. I durst have denied that before you were so choleric.

A.S. By what rule, sir ?

D.S. Marry, sir, by a rule as plain as the plain bald pate of father Time himself.

A.S. Let 's hear it.

D.S. There 's no time for a man to recover his hair that 70 grows bald by nature.

A.S. May he not do it by fine and recovery ?

D.S. Yes, to pay a fine for a periwig, and recover the lost hair of another man.

A.S. Why is Time such a niggard of hair, being, as it is, so plentiful an excrement?

D.S. Because it is a blessing that he bestows on beasts, and what he hath scanted men in hair, he hath given them in wit.

A.S. Why, but there's many a man hath more hair than   80 wit.

D.S. Not a man of those but he hath the wit to lose his hair.

A.S. Why, thou didst conclude hairy men plain dealers without wit.

D.S. The plainer dealer, the sooner lost: yet he loseth it in a kind of jollity.

A.S. For what reason?

D.S. For two, and sound ones too.

A.S. Nay, not sound, I pray you.   90

D.S. Sure ones, then.

A.S. Nay, not sure, in a thing falsing.

D.S. Certain ones, then.

A.S. Name them.

D.S. The one, to save the money that he spends in tiring; the other, that at dinner they should not drop in his porridge.

A.S. You would all this time have prov'd there is no time for all things.

21

*D.S.*Marry, and did, sir ; namely, e'en no time to recover 100
    hair lost by nature.

*A.S.*But your reason was not substantial, why there is no
    time to recover.

*D.S.*Thus I mend it : Time himself is bald, and therefore
    to the world's end will have bald followers.

*A.S.*I knew 'twould be a bald conclusion :
    But, soft ! who wafts us yonder ?

            Enter Adriana and Luciana

*Adr.*Ay, ay, Antipholus, look strange and frown :
    Some other mistress hath thy sweet aspects ;
    I am not Adriana, nor thy wife. 110
    The time was once when thou unurg'd wouldst vow
    That never words were music to thine ear,
    That never object pleasing in thine eye,
    That never touch well welcome to thy hand,
    That never meat sweet-savour'd in thy taste,
    Unless I spake, or look'd, or touch'd, or carv'd to
        thee.
    How comes it now, my husband, O, how comes it,
    That thou art then estranged from thyself ?
    Thyself I call it, being strange to me,
    That, undividable, incorporate, 120
    Am better than thy dear self's better part.
    Ah, do not tear away thyself from me !

For know, my love; as easy mayst thou fall
A drop of water in the breaking gulf,
And take unmingled thence that drop again,
Without addition or diminishing,
As take from me thyself, and not me too.
How dearly would it touch thee to the quick,
Shouldst thou but hear I were licentious?
And that this body, consecrate to thee,   130
By ruffian lust should be contaminate?
Wouldst thou not spit at me, and spurn at me,
And hurl the name of husband in my face,
And tear the stain'd skin of my harlot-brow,
And from my false hand cut the wedding-ring,
And break it with a deep-divorcing vow?
I know thou canst, and therefore see thou do it.
I am possess'd with an adulterate blot,
My blood is mingled with the crime of lust: †
For if we two be one, and thou play false,   140
I do digest the poison of thy flesh,
Being strumpeted by thy contagion.
Keep then fair league and truce with thy true bed,
I live distain'd, thou undishonoured.   ✦

A.S. Plead you to me, fair dame? I know you not:
In Ephesus I am but two hours old,
As strange unto your town as to your talk,

Who, every word by all my wit being scann'd,
Wants wit in all, one word to understand.

Luc. Fie, brother! how the world is chang'd with you! 150
When were you wont to use my sister thus?
She sent for you by Dromio home to dinner.

A.S. By Dromio?

D.S. By me?

Adr. By thee, and this thou didst return from him,
That he did buffet thee, and, in his blows,
Denied my house for his, me for his wife.

A.S. Did you converse, sir, with this gentlewoman?
What is the course and drift of your compact?

D.S. I, sir?   I never saw her till this time. 160

A.S. Villain, thou liest, for even her very words
Didst thou deliver to me on the mart.

D.S. I never spake with her in all my life.

A.S. How can she thus then call us by our names?
Unless it be by inspiration.

Adr. How ill agrees it with your gravity
To counterfeit thus grossly with your slave,
Abetting him to thwart me in my mood!
Be it my wrong, you are from me exempt,
But wrong not that wrong with a more contempt. 170
Come, I will fasten on this sleeve of thine:
Thou art an elm, my husband, I a vine;

Whose weakness, married to thy stronger state,
Makes me with thy strength to communicate :
If aught possess thee from me, it is dross,
Usurping ivy, brier, or idle moss,
Who, all for want of pruning, with intrusion
Infect thy sap, and live on thy confusion.

A.S. To me she speaks ; she moves me for her theme :
What, was I married to her in my dream ?   180
Or sleep I now, and think I hear all this ?
What error drives our eyes and ears amiss ?
Until I know this sure uncertainty,
I 'll entertain the offer'd fallacy.

Luc. Dromio, go bid the servants spread for dinner.

D.S. O, for my beads !   I cross me for a sinner.
This is the fairy land : O spite of spites !
We talk with goblins, owls, and sprites :
If we obey them not, this will ensue,
They 'll suck our breath, or pinch us black and blue. 190

Luc. Why prat'st thou to thyself, and answer'st not ?
Dromio, thou drone, thou snail, thou slug, thou sot !

D.S. I am transformed, master, am not I ?

A.S. I think thou art in mind, and so am I.

D.S. Nay, master, both in mind and in my shape.

A.S. Thou hast thine own form.

D.S.   No, I am an ape.

25

Luc. If thou art chang'd to aught, 'tis to an ass.

D.S. 'Tis true, she rides me, and I long for grass.
　　　'Tis so, I am an ass, else it could never be
　　　But I should know her as well as she knows me.　　200

Adr. Come, come, no longer will I be a fool,
　　　To put the finger in the eye and weep ;
　　　Whilst man and master laughs my woes to scorn.
　　　Come, sir, to dinner ; Dromio, keep the gate.
　　　Husband, I 'll dine above with you to-day,　　　†
　　　And shrive you of a thousand idle pranks.
　　　Sirrah, if any ask you for your master,
　　　Say he dines forth, and let no creature enter.
　　　Come, sister ; Dromio, play the porter well.

A.S. Am I in earth, in heaven, or in hell ?　　210
　　　Sleeping or waking, mad or well-advised ?
　　　Known unto these, and to myself disguised !
　　　I 'll say as they say, and persever so ;
　　　And in this mist at all adventures go.

D.S. Master, shall I be porter at the gate ?

Adr. Ay, and let none enter, lest I break your pate.

Luc. Come, come, Antipholus, we dine too late.　　*Exeunt*

Act Third

SCENES I AND II

Before the house of Antipholus of Ephesus

*Enter Antipholus of Ephesus, Dromio of Ephesus, Angelo,
and Balthazar*

A.E. Good Signior Angelo, you must excuse us all,
    My wife is shrewish when I keep not hours :
    Say that I linger'd with you at your shop
    To see the making of her carcanet,
    And that to-morrow you will bring it home.
    But here's a villain that would face me down
    He met me on the mart, and that I beat him,
    And charg'd him with a thousand marks in gold,
    And that I did deny my wife and house ;
    Thou drunkard, thou, what didst thou mean by this ?   10
D.E. Say what you will, sir, but I know what I know,
    That you beat me at the mart, I have your hand to
        show :
    If the skin were parchment, and the blows you gave
        were ink,
    Your own handwriting would tell you what I think.
A.E. I think thou art an ass.

D.E.   Marry, so it doth appear
        By the wrongs I suffer, and the blows I bear.
        I should kick, being kick'd, and being at that pass,
        You would keep from my heels, and beware of an ass.

A.E. You 're sad, Signior Balthazar : pray God our cheer
        May answer my good will, and your good welcome
                here.   20

Bal. I hold your dainties cheap, sir, and your welcome dear.

A.E. O, Signior Balthazar, either at flesh or fish,
        A table full of welcome makes scarce one dainty dish.

Bal. Good meat, sir, is common, that every churl affords.

A.E. And welcome more common, for that 's nothing but
                words.

Bal. Small cheer and great welcome makes a merry feast.

A.E. Ay, to a niggardly host, and more sparing guest :
        But though my cates be mean, take them in good
                part,
        Better cheer may you have, but not with better heart.
        But, soft ! my door is lock'd.—Go bid them let us in.   30

D.E. Maud, Bridget, Marian, Cicely, Gillian, Ginn !

D.S. (*within*) Mome, malt-horse, capon, coxcomb, idiot,
                patch !
        Either get thee from the door, or sit down at the hatch.
        Dost thou conjure for wenches, that thou call'st for
                such store,

28

When one is one too many ?   Go get thee from the
    door.

D.E. What patch is made our porter ?   My master stays
    in the street.

D.S. (within) Let him walk from whence he came, lest he
    catch cold on 's feet.

A.E. Who talks within there ? ho, open the door !

D.S. (within) Right, sir, I 'll tell you when, an you 'll tell
    me wherefore.

A.E. Wherefore ? for my dinner : I have not din'd to-day.   40

D.S. (within) Nor to-day here you must not, come again
    when you may.

A.E. What art thou that keep'st me out from the house I
    owe ?

D.S. (within) The porter for this time, sir, and my name is
    Dromio.

D.E. O villain, thou hast stolen both mine office and my
    name !
    The one ne'er got me credit, the other mickle blame :
    If thou hadst been Dromio to-day in my place,
    Thou wouldst have chang'd thy face for a name, or
        thy name for an ass.

Luce. (above) What a coil is there, Dromio ? who are those †
    at the gate !

D.E. Let my master in, Luce.

29

Luce.   'Faith, no, he comes too late,
    And so tell your master.

D.E.   O Lord, I must laugh !   50
    Have at you with a proverb ;—Shall I set in my staff ?

*Luce.*Have at you with another, that's,—When ? can you
    tell ?

D.S. (*within*) If thy name be call'd Luce,—Luce, thou hast
    answer'd him well.

*A.E.*Do you hear, you minion ? you 'll let us in, I hope ?

*Luce.*I thought to have ask'd you.

D.S.   (*within*) And you said no.

*D.E.*So, come, help, well struck ! there was blow for
    blow.

*A.E.*Thou baggage, let me in.

Luce.   Can you tell for whose sake ?

*D.E.*Master, knock the door hard.

Luce.   Let him knock till it ache.

*A.E.*You 'll cry for this, minion, if I beat the door down.

*Luce.*What needs all that, and a pair of stocks in the town ?

Adr.(*above*) Who is that at the door that keeps all this
    noise ?   61

D.S. (*within*) By my troth, your town is troubled with
    unruly boys.

*A.E.*Are you there, wife ? you might have come before.

*Adr.*Your wife, sir knave ? go get you from the door.

D.E. If you went in pain, master, this ' knave ' would go
  sore.

Ang. Here is neither cheer, sir, nor welcome : we would
  fain have either.

Bal. In debating which was best, we shall part with
  neither.

D.E. They stand at the door, master, bid them welcome
  hither.

A.E. There is something in the wind, that we cannot
  get in.

D.E. You would say so, master if your garments were thin.   70
  Your cake here is warm within ; you stand here in the
    cold :
  It would make a man mad as a buck, to be so bought
    and sold.

A.E. Go fetch me something, I 'll break ope the gate.

D.S. (*within*) Break any breaking here, and I 'll break your
  knave's pate.

D.E. A man may break a word with you, sir ; and words are
  but wind ;
  Ay, and break it in your face, so he break it not behind.

D.S. (*within*) It seems thou want'st breaking ; out upon
  thee, hind !

D.E. Here 's too much ' out upon thee ! ' I pray thee, let
  me in.

31

D.S. (within) Ay, when fowls have no feathers, and fish have
    no fin.

A.E. Well, I 'll break in: go borrow me a crow.   80

D.E. A crow without feather?   Master, mean you so
    For a fish without a fin, there's a fowl without a
        feather:
    If a crow help us in, sirrah, we 'll pluck a crow together.

A.E. Go get thee gone, fetch me an iron crow.

Bal. Have patience, sir: O, let it not be so!
    Herein you war against your reputation,
    And draw within the compass of suspect
    The unviolated honour of your wife.
    Once this,—your long experience of her wisdom,
    Her sober virtue, years, and modesty,   90
    Plead on her part some cause to you unknown;
    And doubt not, sir, but she will well excuse
    Why at this time the doors are made against you.
    Be rul'd by me: depart in patience,
    And let us to the Tiger all to dinner,
    And about evening come yourself alone,
    To know the reason of this strange restraint.
    If by strong hand you offer to break in
    Now in the stirring passage of the day,
    A vulgar comment will be made of it;   100
    And that supposed by the common rout

Against your yet ungalled estimation,
That may with foul intrusion enter in,
And dwell upon your grave when you are dead;
For slander lives upon succession,
For ever hous'd where it gets possession.

A.E. You have prevail'd; I will depart in quiet,
And, in despite of mirth, mean to be merry.
I know a wench of excellent discourse,
Pretty and witty; wild, and yet, too, gentle: 110
There will we dine. This woman that I mean,
My wife—but I protest without desert—
Hath oftentimes upbraided me withal:
To her will we to dinner. (*to Ang.*) Get you home,
And fetch the chain; by this I know 'tis made:
Bring it, I pray you, to the Porpentine;
For there's the house: that chain will I bestow
(Be it for nothing but to spite my wife)
Upon mine hostess there; good sir, make haste.
Since mine own doors refuse to entertain me,   120
I'll knock elsewhere, to see if they'll disdain me.

Ang. I'll meet you at that place some hour hence.

A.E. Do so. This jest shall cost me some expense.

         Exeunt

Enter Luciana, with Antipholus of Syracuse

Luc. And may it be that you have quite forgot
    A husband's office? shall, Antipholus,
Even in the spring of love, thy love-springs rot?
    Shall love, in building, grow so ruinate?   †
If you did wed my sister for her wealth,
    Then for her wealth's sake use her with more
      kindness:
Or if you like elsewhere, do it by stealth;
    Muffle your false love with some show of
      blindness:
Let not my sister read it in your eye;
    Be not thy tongue thy own shame's orator;   10
Look sweet, speak fair, become disloyalty;
    Apparel vice like virtue's harbinger;
Bear a fair presence, though your heart be tainted;
    Teach sin the carriage of a holy saint;
Be secret-false: what need she be acquainted?
    What simple thief brags of his own attaint?
'Tis double wrong, to truant with your bed,
    And let her read it in thy looks at board:

Shame hath a bastard fame, well managed;
　　Ill deeds is doubled with an evil word.　　　　20
Alas, poor women! make us but believe,
　　(Being compact of credit) that you love us;
Though others have the arm, show us the sleeve;
　　We in your motion turn, and you may move us.
Then, gentle brother, get you in again;
　　Comfort my sister, cheer her, call her wife;
'Tis holy sport, to be a little vain,
　　When the sweet breath of flattery conquers strife.

*A.S.*Sweet mistress,—what your name is else, I know not,
　　Nor by what wonder you do hit of mine,—　　30
　　Less in your knowledge and your grace you show
　　　　not
　　Than our earth's wonder, more than earth divine.
Teach me, dear creature, how to think and speak;
　　Lay open to my earthy-gross conceit,
Smother'd in errors, feeble, shallow, weak,
　　The folded meaning of your words' deceit.
Against my soul's pure truth why labour you,
　　To make it wander in an unknown field?
Are you a god? would you create me new?
　　Transform me then, and to your power I'll yield.　40
But if that I am I, then well I know
　　Your weeping sister is no wife of mine,

35

Nor to her bed no homage do I owe :
　　Far more, far more to you do I decline.
O, train me not, sweet mermaid, with thy note,
　　To drown me in thy sister's flood of tears :
Sing, siren, for thyself, and I will dote :
　　Spread o'er the silver waves thy golden hairs ;
And as a bed I 'll take them, and there lie ;
　　And, in that glorious supposition, think　　　　50
He gains by death that hath such means to die :
　　Let Love, being light, be drowned if she sink !

Luc. What, are you mad, that you do reason so ?

A.S. Not mad, but mated, how, I do not know.

Luc. It is a fault that springeth from your eye.

A.S. For gazing on your beams, fair sun, being by.

Luc. Gaze where you should, and that will clear your sight.

A.S. As good to wink, sweet love, as look on night.

Luc. Why call you me love ? call my sister so.

A.S. Thy sister's sister.

Luc. 　　　　　　That 's my sister.

A.S. 　　　　　　　　　　No ;　　　　　　　　60
　　It is thyself, mine own self's better part ;
　　Mine eye's clear eye, my dear heart's dearer heart ;
　　My food, my fortune, and my sweet hope's aim ;
　　My sole earth's heaven, and my heaven's claim.

Luc. All this my sister is, or else should be.

A.S. Call thyself sister, sweet, for I am thee.
　　　Thee will I love, and with thee lead my life :
　　　Thou hast no husband yet, nor I no wife.
　　　Give me thy hand.

Luc. 　　　　　　O, soft, sir ! hold you still :
　　　I 'll fetch my sister, to get her good will.　　*Exit* 70

Enter Dromio of Syracuse

A.S. Why, how now, Dromio ! where runn'st thou so fast ?

D.S. Do you know me, sir ? am I Dromio ? am I your
　　　man ? am I myself ?

A.S. Thou art Dromio, thou art my man, thou art thyself.

D.S. I am an ass, I am a woman's man, and besides myself.

A.S. What woman's man ? and how besides thyself ?

D.S. Marry, sir, besides myself, I am due to a woman ; one
　　　that claims me, one that haunts me, one that will have me.

A.S. What claim lays she to thee ?

D.S. Marry, sir, such claim as you would lay to your horse,　80
　　　and she would have me as a beast, not that, I being a
　　　beast, she would have me, but that she, being a very
　　　beastly creature, lays claim to me.

A.S. What is she ?

D.S. A very reverent body ; ay, such a one as a man may
　　　not speak of, without he say Sir-reverence.　I have
　　　but lean luck in the match, and yet is she a wondrous
　　　fat marriage.

37

A.S. How dost thou mean a fat marriage?

D.S. Marry, sir, she 's the kitchen-wench, and all grease, 90
and I know not what use to put her to, but to make a
lamp of her, and run from her by her own light. I
warrant, her rags, and the tallow in them, will burn
a Poland winter: if she lives till doomsday, she 'll
burn a week longer than the whole world.

A.S. What complexion is she of?

D.S. Swart, like my shoe, but her face nothing like so
clean kept: for why? she sweats; a man may go
over shoes in the grime of it.

A.S. That 's a fault that water will mend. 100

D.S. No, sir, 'tis in grain; Noah's flood could not do it.

A.S. What 's her name?

D.S. Nell, sir; but her name and three quarters, that 's an
ell and three quarters, will not measure her from hip
to hip.

A.S. Then she bears some breadth?

D.S. No longer from head to foot than from hip to hip:
she is spherical, like a globe; I could find out
countries in her.

A.S. In what part of her body stands Ireland? 110

D.S. Marry, sir, in her buttocks: I found it out by the
bogs.

A.S. Where Scotland?

D.S. I found it by the barrenness, hard in the palm of the hand.

A.S. Where France ?

D.S. In her forehead, arm'd and reverted, making war against her heir.   †

A.S. Where England ?

D.S. I looked for the chalky cliffs, but I could find no †
whiteness in them ; but I guess it stood in her chin, 121
by the salt rheum that ran between France and it.

A.S. Where Spain ?

D.S. 'Faith, I saw it not ; but I felt it hot in her breath.

A.S. Where America, the Indies ?

D.S. Oh, sir, upon her nose, all o'er embellished with
rubies, carbuncles, sapphires, declining their rich
aspect to the hot breath of Spain ; who sent whole
armadoes of carracks to be ballast at her nose.

A.S. Where stood Belgia, the Netherlands ?   130

D.S. Oh, sir, I did not look so low. To conclude, this
drudge or diviner laid claim to me, called me Dromio,
swore I was assur'd to her, told me what privy marks
I had about me, as the mark of my shoulder, the mole
in my neck, the great wart on my left arm, that I,
amaz'd, ran from her as a witch :

And, I think, if my breast had not been made of
faith, and my heart of steel,

   She had transform'd me to a curtal dog, and made me
    turn i' the wheel.   140

A.S. Go hie thee presently post to the road :
   An if the wind blow any way from shore,
   I will not harbour in this town to-night :
   If any bark put forth, come to the mart,
   Where I will walk till thou return to me.
   If every one knows us, and we know none,
   'Tis time, I think, to trudge, pack, and be gone.

D.S. As from a bear a man would run for life,
   So fly I from her that would be my wife. *Exit*

A.S. There 's none but witches do inhabit here ; 150
   And therefore 'tis high time that I were hence.
   She that doth call me husband, even my soul
   Doth for a wife abhor. But her fair sister,
   Possess'd with such a gentle sovereign grace,
   Of such enchanting presence and discourse,
   Hath almost made me traitor to myself :
   But, lest myself be guilty to self-wrong,
   I 'll stop mine ears against the mermaid's song.

      Enter Angelo with the chain

Ang. Master Antipholus,—

A.S.   Ay, that 's my name.

Ang. I know it well, sir : lo, here is the chain ; 160
   I thought to have ta'en you at the Porpentine,

The chain unfinish'd made me stay thus long.

A.S. What is your will that I shall do with this?

Ang. What please yourself, sir: I have made it for you.

A.S. Made it for me, sir? I bespoke it not.

Ang. Not once, nor twice, but twenty times you have:
   Go home with it, and please your wife withal,
   And soon at supper-time I'll visit you,
   And then receive my money for the chain.

A.S. I pray you, sir, receive the money now,   170
   For fear you ne'er see chain nor money more.

Ang. You are a merry man, sir, fare you well.   *Exit*

A.S. What I should think of this, I cannot tell:
   But this I think, there's no man is so vain
   That would refuse so fair an offer'd chain.
   I see a man here needs not live by shifts,
   When in the streets he meets such golden gifts:
   I'll to the mart, and there for Dromio stay:
   If any ship put out, then straight away.   *Exit*

Act Fourth

SCENE I

A public place

Enter Second Merchant, Angelo, and an Officer

2.M. You know since Pentecost the sum is due,
　　　And since I have not much importun'd you,
　　　Nor now I had not, but that I am bound
　　　To Persia, and want guilders for my voyage :
　　　Therefore make present satisfaction,
　　　Or I 'll attach you by this officer.

Ang. Even just the sum that I do owe to you
　　　Is growing to me by Antipholus,
　　　And in the instant that I met with you
　　　He had of me a chain ; at five o'clock　　　　10
　　　I shall receive the money for the same :
　　　Pleaseth you walk with me down to his house,
　　　I will discharge my bond, and thank you too.

　　　*Enter Antipholus of Ephesus and Dromio of Ephesus
　　　　　　from the Courtezan's*

Off. That labour may you save : see where he comes.

A.E. While I go to the goldsmith's house, go thou
　　　And buy a rope's end ; that will I bestow

42

  Among my wife and their confederates,
  For locking me out of my doors by day.
  But soft, I see the goldsmith ; get thee gone,
  Buy thou a rope, and bring it home to me.   20
*D.E.*I buy a thousand pound a year : I buy a rope. *Exit*
*A.E.*A man is well holp up that trusts to you :
  I promised your presence, and the chain,
  But neither chain nor goldsmith came to me :
  Belike you thought our love would last too long,
  If it were chain'd together ; and therefore came not.
*Ang.*Saving your merry humour, here 's the note
  How much your chain weighs to the utmost carat,
  The fineness of the gold, and chargeful fashion,
  Which doth amount to three odd ducats more 30
  Than I stand debted to this gentleman :
  I pray you, see him presently discharg'd,
  For he is bound to sea, and stays but for it.
*A.E.*I am not furnish'd with the present money ;
  Besides, I have some business in the town.
  Good signior, take the stranger to my house,
  And with you take the chain, and bid my wife
  Disburse the sum, on the receipt thereof ;
  Perchance I will be there as soon as you.
*Ang.*Then you will bring the chain to her yourself ? 40
*A.E.*No ; bear it with you, lest I come not time enough.

*Ang.*Well, sir, I will.   Have you the chain about you?

*A.E.*An if I have not, sir, I hope you have ;

Or else you may return without your money.

*Ang.*Nay, come, I pray you, sir, give me the chain :

Both wind and tide stays for this gentleman,

And I, to blame, have held him here too long.

*A.E.*Good Lord ! you use this dalliance to excuse

Your breach of promise to the Porpentine.

I should have chid you for not bringing it,   50

But, like a shrew, you first began to brawl.

*2.M.*The hour steals on ; I pray you, sir, dispatch.

*Ang.*You hear how he importunes me ;—the chain !

*A.E.*Why, give it to my wife, and fetch your money.

*Ang.*Come, come, you know I gave it you even now.

Either send the chain, or send by me some token.   †

*A.E.*Fie, now you run this humour out of breath ;

Come, where's the chain ?   I pray you, let me see it.

*2.M.*My business cannot brook this dalliance.

Good sir, say whether you'll answer me, or no :   60

If not, I'll leave him to the officer.

*A.E.*I answer you ? what should I answer you ?

*Ang.*The money that you owe me for the chain.

*A.E.*I owe you none, till I receive the chain.

*Ang.*You know I gave it you half an hour since.

*A.E.*You gave me none : you wrong me much to say so.

*Ang.*You wrong me more, sir, in denying it :
Consider how it stands upon my credit.

2.*M.* Well, officer, arrest him at my suit.

Off. I do, and charge you in the duke's name to obey me.   70

*Ang.*This touches me in reputation.
Either consent to pay this sum for me,
Or I attach you by this officer.

*A.E.*Consent to pay thee that I never had ?
Arrest me, foolish fellow, if thou dar'st.

*Ang.*Here is thy fee, arrest him, officer.
I would not spare my brother in this case,
If he should scorn me so apparently.

Off. I do arrest you, sir ; you hear the suit.

*A.E.*I do obey thee, till I give thee bail.   80
But, sirrah, you shall buy this sport as dear
As all the metal in your shop will answer.

*Ang.*Sir, sir, I shall have law in Ephesus,
To your notorious shame, I doubt it not.

Enter Dromio of Syracuse, from the bay

D.S. Master, there is a bark of Epidamnum
That stays but till her owner comes aboard,
And then, sir, she bears away.   Our fraughtage, sir,
I have convey'd aboard, and I have bought
The oil, the balsamum, and aqua-vitæ.
The ship is in her trim, the merry wind   90

  Blows fair from land : they stay for nought at all
  But for their owner, master, and yourself.
*A.E.*How now ? a madman ? Why, thou peevish sheep,
  What ship of Epidamnum stays for me ?
D.S. A ship you sent me to, to hire waftage.
*A.E.*Thou drunken slave, I sent thee for a rope,
  And told thee to what purpose, and what end.
D.S. You sent me for a rope's end as soon :
  You sent me to the bay, sir, for a bark.
*A.E.*I will debate this matter at more leisure,   100
  And teach your ears to list me with more heed.
  To Adriana, villain, hie thee straight :
  Give her this key, and tell her, in the desk
  That's cover'd o'er with Turkish tapestry
  There is a purse of ducats ; let her send it :
  Tell her I am arrested in the street,
  And that shall bail me : hie thee, slave, be gone !
  On, officer, to prison, till it come.
    Exeunt Sec. Merchant, Angelo, Officer, and A. E.
D.S. To Adriana ? that is where we din'd,
  Where Dowsabel did claim me for her husband : 110
  She is too big, I hope, for me to compass.
  Thither I must, although against my will ;
  For servants must their masters' minds fulfil. *Exit*

SCENE II

The house of Antipholus of Ephesus

Enter Adriana and Luciana

Adr. Ah, Luciana, did he tempt thee so?
> Mightst thou perceive austerely in his eye
> That he did plead in earnest, yea or no?
> Look'd he or red or pale, or sad or merrily?
> What observation mad'st thou in this case,
> Of his heart's meteors tilting in his face?

Luc. First he denied you had in him no right.

Adr. He meant he did me none; the more my spite.

Luc. Then swore he that he was a stranger here.

Adr. And true he swore, though yet forsworn he were.   10

Luc. Then pleaded I for you.

>   And what said he?

Luc. That love I begg'd for you he begg'd of me.

Adr. With what persuasion did he tempt thy love?

Luc. With words that in an honest suit might move,
> First he did praise my beauty, then my speech.

Adr. Didst speak him fair?

Luc.   Have patience, I beseech.

Adr. I cannot, nor I will not, hold me still;
> My tongue, though not my heart, shall have his will.
> He is deformed, crooked, old, and sere,

Ill-fac'd, worse bodied, shapeless everywhere; 20
Vicious, ungentle, foolish, blunt, unkind,
Stigmatical in making, worse in mind.

Luc. Who would be jealous, then, of such a one?
No evil lost is wail'd when it is gone.

Adr. Ah, but I think him better than I say;
And yet would herein others' eyes were worse.
Far from her nest the lapwing cries away:
My heart prays for him, though my tongue do curse.

Enter Dromio of Syracuse

D.S. Here! go; the desk, the purse! sweet, now, make †
haste.

Luc. How hast thou lost thy breath?

D.S.   By running fast. 30

Adr. Where is thy master, Dromio? is he well?

D.S. No, he's in Tartar limbo, worse than hell.
A devil in an everlasting garment hath him;
One whose hard heart is button'd up with steel;
A fiend, a fairy, pitiless and rough;   †
A wolf, nay, worse, a fellow all in buff;
A back-friend, a shoulder-clapper, one that counter-
mands
The passages of alleys, creeks, and narrow lands;
A hound that runs counter, and yet draws dry-foot
well;

48

One that before the Judgement carries poor souls to
    hell.   40

Adr. Why, man, what is the matter?

D.S. I do not know the matter: he is 'rested on the case.

Adr. What, is he arrested?   Tell me at whose suit.

D.S. I know not at whose suit he is arrested well;
    But he's in a suit of buff which 'rested him, that can I tell.
    Will you send him, Mistress Redemption, the money †
      in his desk?

Adr. Go fetch it, sister.   (*exit Luciana.*)   This I wonder at,
    That he, unknown to me, should be in debt.
    Tell me, was he arrested on a band?

D.S. Not on a band, but on a stronger thing;   50
    A chain, a chain!   Do you not hear it ring?

Adr. What, the chain?

D.S. No, no, the bell, 'tis time that I were gone:
    It was two ere I left him, and now the clock strikes
      one.

Adr. The hours come back! that did I never hear.

D.S. O, yes; if any hour meet a sergeant, 'a turns back for
      very fear.

Adr. As if Time were in debt! how fondly dost thou
      reason!

D.S. Time is a very bankrupt, and owes more than he's
      worth to season.

Nay, he's a thief too : have you not heard men say,
That Time comes stealing on by night and day ?   60
If Time be in debt and theft, and a sergeant in the way,
Hath he not reason to turn back an hour in a day ?

Re-enter Luciana with a purse

Adr. Go, Dromio, there's the money, bear it straight,
    And bring thy master home immediately.
    Come, sister : I am press'd down with conceit,—
    Conceit, my comfort and my injury.   *Exeunt*

SCENES III AND IV

A public place

Enter Antipholus of Syracuse

A.S. There's not a man I meet but doth salute me
    As if I were their well-acquainted friend,
    And every one doth call me by my name :
    Some tender money to me, some invite me ;
    Some other give me thanks for kindness ;
    Some offer me commodities to buy :
    Even now a tailor call'd me in his shop,
    And show'd me silks that he had bought for me,
    And therewithal took measure of my body.

Sure, these are but imaginary wiles,   10
And Lapland sorcerers inhabit here.

Enter Dromio of Syracuse

D.S. Master, here's the gold you sent me for.

What, have you got the picture of old Adam new- †
apparell'd ?

A.S. What gold is this ? what Adam dost thou mean ?

D.S. Not that Adam that kept the Paradise ; but that Adam
that keeps the prison : he that goes in the calf's
skin, that was kill'd for the Prodigal ; he that came
behind you, sir, like an evil angel, and bid you for-
sake your liberty.   20

A.S. I understand thee not.

D.S. No ? why, 'tis a plain case : he that went, like a †
base-viol, in a case of leather ; the man, sir, that,
when gentlemen are tir'd, gives them a sob, and
'rests them ; he, sir, that takes pity on decay'd men,
and gives them suits of durance ; he that sets up his
rest to do more exploits with his mace than a morris-
pike.

A.S. What, thou meanest an officer ?

D.S. Ay, sir, the sergeant of the band ; he that brings any   30
man to answer it that breaks his band ; one that
thinks a man always going to bed, and says, ' God
give you good rest ! '

A.S. Well, sir, there rest in your foolery. Is there any
　　　ship puts forth to-night ? may we be gone ?

D.S. Why, sir, I brought you word an hour since, that the
　　　bark Expedition put forth to-night, and then were
　　　you hinder'd by the sergeant, to tarry for the hoy
　　　Delay. Here are the angels that you sent for to
　　　deliver you.　　　　　　　　　　　　　　　　　　40

A.S. The fellow is distract, and so am I,
　　　And here we wander in illusions :
　　　Some blessed power deliver us from hence !

Enter a Courtezan

Cou. Well met, well met, Master Antipholus,
　　　I see, sir, you have found the goldsmith now :
　　　Is that the chain you promis'd me to-day ?

A.S. Satan, avoid ! I charge thee, tempt me not.

D.S. Master, is this Mistress Satan ?

A.S. It is the devil.

D.S. Nay, she is worse, she is the devil's dam ; and here　50
　　　she comes in the habit of a light wench, and thereof
　　　comes that the wenches say, ' God damn me ; ' that 's
　　　as much to say, ' God make me a light wench.' It
　　　is written, they appear to men like angels of light,
　　　light is an effect of fire, and fire will burn ;
　　　ergo, light wenches will burn. Come not near
　　　her.

Cou. Your man and you are marvellous merry, sir.

  Will you go with me ?   We 'll mend our dinner here.

D.S. Master, if you do, expect spoon-meat, or bespeak a 60

  long spoon.   †

A.S. Why, Dromio ?

D.S. Marry, he must have a long spoon that must eat

  with the devil.

A.S. Avoid then, fiend ! what tell'st thou me of supping ?

  Thou art, as you are all, a sorceress :

  I conjure you to leave me and be gone.

Cou. Give me the ring of mine you had at dinner,

  Or for my diamond the chain you promis'd,

  And I 'll be gone, sir, and not trouble you. 70

D.S. Some devils ask but the parings of one's nail,

  A rush, a hair, a drop of blood, a pin,

  A nut, a cherry-stone ;

  But she, more covetous, would have a chain.

  Master, be wise ; an if you give it her,

  The devil will shake her chain, and fright us with it.

Cou. I pray you, sir, my ring, or else the chain ;

  I hope you do not mean to cheat me so.

A.S. Avaunt, thou witch !   Come, Dromio, let us go.

D.S. 'Fly pride,' says the peacock : mistress, that you

    know.   *Exeunt A. S. and D. S.* 80

Cou. Now, out of doubt Antipholus is mad,

Else would he never so demean himself.
A ring he hath of mine worth forty ducats,
And for the same he promised me a chain:
Both one and other he denies me now.
The reason that I gather he is mad,
Besides this present instance of his rage,
Is a mad tale he told to-day at dinner,
Of his own doors being shut against his entrance.
Belike his wife, acquainted with his fits,   90
On purpose shut the doors against his way.
My way is now to hie home to his house,
And tell his wife that, being lunatic,
He rush'd into my house, and took perforce
My ring away.   This course I fittest choose;
For forty ducats is too much to lose.   *Exit*

Enter Antipholus of Ephesus and the Officer

*A.E.*Fear me not, man; I will not break away:
I'll give thee, ere I leave thee, so much money,
To warrant thee, as I am 'rested for.
My wife is in a wayward mood to-day,

And will not lightly trust the messenger.
That I should be attach'd in Ephesus,
I tell you, 'twill sound harshly in her ears.

Enter Dromio of Ephesus with a rope's-end

Here comes my man, I think he brings the money.
How now, sir ? have you that I sent you for ?

D.E. Here's that, I warrant you, will pay them all.   10

A.E. But where's the money ?

D.E. Why, sir, I gave the money for the rope.

A.E. Five hundred ducats, villain, for a rope ?

D.E. I'll serve you, sir, five hundred at the rate.

A.E. To what end did I bid thee hie thee home ?

D.E. To a rope's-end, sir ; and to that end am I return'd.

A.E. And to that end, sir, I will welcome you.   *Beating him*

Off. Good sir, be patient.

D.E. Nay, 'tis for me to be patient, I am in adversity.

Off. Good now, hold thy tongue.   20

D.E. Nay, rather persuade him to hold his hands.

A.E. Thou whoreson, senseless villain !

D.E. I would I were senseless, sir, that I might not feel
     your blows.

A.E. Thou art sensible in nothing but blows, and so is an
     ass.

D.E. I am an ass, indeed, you may prove it by my long
     ears. I have serv'd him from the hour of my

e   55

nativity to this instant, and have nothing at his
hands for my service but blows. When I am cold,   30
he heats me with beating; when I am warm, he cools
me with beating: I am wak'd with it when I sleep,
rais'd with it when I sit, driven out of doors with it
when I go from home, welcom'd home with it when
I return, nay, I bear it on my shoulders, as a beggar
wont her brat; and, I think, when he hath lam'd
me, I shall beg with it from door to door.

*A.E.*Come, go along; my wife is coming yonder.

    Enter Adriana, Luciana, the Courtezan, and Pinch

*D.E.*Mistress, '*respice finem*,' respect your end, or rather,
the prophecy like the parrot, 'beware the rope's-   40
end.'

*A.E.*Wilt thou still talk?   *Beating him*

Cou. How say you now? is not your husband mad?

*Adr.*His incivility confirms no less.

    Good Doctor Pinch, you are a conjurer,
    Establish him in his true sense again,
    And I will please you what you will demand.

Luc. Alas, how fiery and how sharp he looks!

Cou. Mark, how he trembles in his ecstasy!

Pin. Give me your hand, and let me feel your pulse.   50

*A.E.*There is my hand, and let it feel your ear.

                    Striking him

Pin. I charge thee, Satan, hous'd within this man,
  To yield possession to my holy prayers,
  And to thy state of darkness hie thee straight.
  I conjure thee by all the saints in heaven !

A.E. Peace, doting wizard, peace ! I am not mad.

Adr. O, that thou wert not, poor distressed soul !

A.E. You minion, you, are these your customers ?
  Did this companion with the saffron face
  Revel and feast it at my house to-day,   60
  Whilst upon me the guilty doors were shut,
  And I denied to enter in my house ?

Adr. O husband, God doth know you din'd at home ;
  Where would you had remain'd until this time,
  Free from these slanders, and this open shame !

A.E. Din'd at home !   Thou villain, what sayest thou ?

D.E. Sir, sooth to say, you did not dine at home.

A.E. Were not my doors lock'd up, and I shut out ?

D.E. Perdie, your doors were lock'd, and you shut out.

A.E. And did not she herself revile me there ?   70

D.E. Sans fable, she herself revil'd you there.

A.E. Did not her kitchen-maid rail, taunt, and scorn me ?

D.E. Certes, she did ; the kitchen-vestal scorn'd you.

A.E. And did not I in rage depart from thence ?

D.E. In verity you did, my bones bear witness,
  That since have felt the vigour of his rage.

*Adr.*Is 't good to soothe him in these contraries ?

Pin. It is no shame, the fellow finds his vein,
    And, yielding to him, humours well his frenzy.

*A.E.*Thou hast suborn'd the goldsmith to arrest me.   80

*Adr.*Alas, I sent you money to redeem you,
    By Dromio here, who came in haste for it.

*D.E.*Money by me ? heart and good-will you might ;
    But surely, master, not a rag of money.

*A.E.*Went'st not thou to her for a purse of ducats ?

*Adr.*He came to me, and I deliver'd it.

Luc. And I am witness with her that she did.

*D.E.*God and the rope-maker bear me witness
    That I was sent for nothing but a rope !

Pin. Mistress, both man and master is possess'd,   90
    I know it by their pale and deadly looks,
    They must be bound, and laid in some dark room.

*A.E.*Say, wherefore didst thou lock me forth to-day,
    And why dost thou deny the bag of gold ?

*Adr.*I did not, gentle husband, lock thee forth.

*D.E.*And, gentle master, I receiv'd no gold ;
    But I confess, sir, that we were lock'd out.

*Adr.*Dissembling villain, thou speak'st false in both.

*A.E.*Dissembling harlot, thou art false in all,
    And art confederate with a damned pack,   100
    To make a loathsome abject scorn of me :

But with these nails I 'll pluck out these false eyes,
That would behold in me this shameful sport.

Enter three or four, and offer to bind him.   He strives

Adr. O, bind him, bind him ! let him not come near me.
Pin. More company ! The fiend is strong within him.
Luc. Ay me, poor man, how pale and wan he looks !
A.E. What, will you murder me ?   Thou gaoler, thou,
    I am thy prisoner : wilt thou suffer them
    To make a rescue ?

Off.   Masters, let him go :
    He is my prisoner, and you shall not have him.   110
Pin. Go bind this man, for he is frantic too.

                         They offer to bind D. E.

Adr. What wilt thou do, thou peevish officer ?
    Hast thou delight to see a wretched man
    Do outrage and displeasure to himself ?
Off. He is my prisoner : if I let him go,
    The debt he owes will be requir'd of me.
Adr. I will discharge thee ere I go from thee :
    Bear me forthwith unto his creditor,
    And, knowing how the debt grows, I will pay it.
    Good master doctor, see him safe convey'd   120
    Home to my house.   O most unhappy day !
A.E. O most unhappy strumpet !
D.E. Master, I am here enter'd in bond for you.

59

A.E. Out on thee, villain! wherefore dost thou mad me?

D.E. Will you be bound for nothing? be mad, good
    master: cry, The devil!

Luc. God help poor souls, how idly do they talk!

Adr. Go bear him hence.   Sister, go you with me.

    Exeunt all but Adriana, Luciana, Officer and Courtezan
    Say now, whose suit is he arrested at?

Off. One Angelo, a goldsmith, do you know him?   130

Adr. I know the man.   What is the sum he owes?

Off. Two hundred ducats.

Adr.   Say, how grows it due?

Off. Due for a chain your husband had of him.

Adr. He did bespeak a chain for me, but had it not.

Cou. When as your husband, all in rage, to-day
    Came to my house, and took away my ring,—
    The ring I saw upon his finger now,—
    Straight after did I meet him with a chain.

Adr. It may be so, but I did never see it.
    Come, gaoler, bring me where the goldsmith is: 140
    I long to know the truth hereof at large.

    Enter Antipholus of Syracuse with his rapier drawn,
          and Dromio of Syracuse

Luc. God, for thy mercy! they are loose again.

Adr. And come with naked swords.
    Let's call more help to have them bound again.

Off. Away ! they 'll kill us.

                    Exeunt all but A. S. and D. S.

A.S. I see these witches are afraid of swords.

D.S. She that would be your wife now ran from you.

A.S. Come to the Centaur, fetch our stuff from thence :
    I long that we were safe and sound aboard.

D.S. Faith, stay here this night, they will surely do us no **150**
    harm : you saw they speak us fair, give us gold :
    methinks they are such a gentle nation, that, but for
    the mountain of mad flesh that claims marriage of
    me, I could find in my heart to stay here still, and
    turn witch.

A.S. I will not stay to-night for all the town ;
    Therefore away, to get our stuff aboard.   *Exeunt*

Act Fifth

SCENE I

A street before a Priory

Enter Second Merchant and Angelo

Ang. I am sorry, sir, that I have hinder'd you,
    But, I protest, he had the chain of me,
    Though most dishonestly he doth deny it.

2.M. How is the man esteem'd here in the city?

Ang. Of very reverent reputation, sir,
  Of credit infinite, highly belov'd,
  Second to none that lives here in the city:
  His word might bear my wealth at any time.

2.M. Speak softly: yonder, as I think, he walks.

  Enter Antipholus of Syracuse and Dromio of Syracuse

Ang. 'Tis so; and that self chain about his neck,   10
  Which he forswore most monstrously to have.
  Good sir, draw near to me, I 'll speak to him;
  Signior Antipholus, I wonder much
  That you would put me to this shame and trouble,
  And not without some scandal to yourself,
  With circumstance and oath so to deny
  This chain, which now you wear so openly:
  Beside the charge, the shame, imprisonment,
  You have done wrong to this my honest friend,
  Who, but for staying on our controversy,   20
  Had hoisted sail, and put to sea to-day:
  This chain you had of me; can you deny it?

A.S. I think I had; I never did deny it.

2.M. Yes, that you did, sir, and forswore it too.

A.S. Who heard me to deny it or forswear it?

2.M. These ears of mine thou know'st did hear thee:
  Fie on thee, wretch! 'tis pity that thou liv'st

62

To walk where any honest men resort.

*A.S.*Thou art a villain to impeach me thus :

I'll prove mine honour, and mine honesty,   30

Against thee presently, if thou dar'st stand.

*2.M.*I dare, and do defy thee for a villain.   *They draw*
Enter Adriana, Luciana, the Courtezan, and others

*Adr.*Hold, hurt him not, for God's sake ! he is mad,

Some get within him, take his sword away :

Bind Dromio too, and bear them to my house.

*D.S.*Run, master, run ; for God's sake, take a house !

This is some priory.   In, or we are spoil'd !

Exeunt A. S. and D. S. to the Priory
Enter the Lady Abbess

*Abb.*Be quiet, people.   Wherefore throng you hither ?

*Adr.*To fetch my poor distracted husband hence,

Let us come in, that we may bind him fast,   40

And bear him home for his recovery.

*Ang.*I knew he was not in his perfect wits.

*2.M.*I am sorry now that I did draw on him.

*Abb.*How long hath this possession held the man ?

*Adr.*This week he hath been heavy, sour sad,

And much different from the man he was ;

But till this afternoon his passion

Ne'er brake into extremity of rage.

*Abb.*Hath he not lost much wealth by wreck of sea ?

Buried some dear friend ?   Hath not else his eye   50
Stray'd his affection in unlawful love,
A sin prevailing much in youthful men,
Who give their eyes the liberty of gazing ?
Which of these sorrows is he subject to ?
*Adr.*To none of these, except it be the last,
Namely, some love that drew him oft from home.
*Abb.*You should for that have reprehended him.
*Adr.*Why, so I did.
Abb.   Ay, but not rough enough.
*Adr.*As roughly as my modesty would let me.
*Abb.*Haply, in private.
Adr.   And in assemblies too.   60
*Abb.*Ay, but not enough.
*Adr.*It was the copy of our conference :
In bed, he slept not for my urging it,
At board, he fed not for my urging it ;
Alone, it was the subject of my theme ;
In company I often glanced it ;
Still did I tell him it was vile and bad.
*Abb.*And thereof came it that the man was mad.
The venom clamours of a jealous woman
Poisons more deadly than a mad dog's tooth.   70
It seems his sleeps were hinder'd by thy railing :
And thereof comes it that his head is light.

Thou say'st his meat was sauc'd with thy upbraidings :
Unquiet meals make ill digestions,
Thereof the raging fire of fever bred,
And what 's a fever but a fit of madness ?
Thou say'st his sports were hinder'd by thy brawls :
Sweet recreation barr'd, what doth ensue
But moody and dull melancholy,
Kinsman to grim and comfortless despair,   80
And at her heels a huge infectious troop
Of pale distemperatures, and foes to life ?
In food, in sport, and life-preserving rest
To be disturb'd, would mad or man or beast :
The consequence is, then, thy jealous fits
Have scar'd thy husband from the use of wits.

Luc. She never reprehended him but mildly,
When he demean'd himself rough, rude, and wildly.
Why bear you these rebukes, and answer not ?

Adr. She did betray me to my own reproof.   90
Good people, enter, and lay hold on him.

Abb. No, not a creature enters in my house.

Adr. Then let your servants bring my husband forth.

Abb. Neither : he took this place for sanctuary,
And it shall privilege him from your hands,
Till I have brought him to his wits again,
Or lose my labour in assaying it.

*Adr.*I will attend my husband, be his nurse,
    Diet his sickness, for it is my office,
    And will have no attorney but myself,   100
    And therefore let me have him home with me.

*Abb.*Be patient, for I will not let him stir
    Till I have us'd the approved means I have,
    With wholesome syrups, drugs, and holy prayers,
    To make of him a formal man again :
    It is a branch and parcel of mine oath,
    A charitable duty of my order ;
    Therefore depart, and leave him here with me.

*Adr.*I will not hence, and leave my husband here :
    And ill it doth beseem your holiness   110
    To separate the husband and the wife.

*Abb.*Be quiet and depart ; thou shalt not have him. *Exit*

Luc. Complain unto the Duke of this indignity.

*Adr.*Come, go ; I will fall prostrate at his feet,
    And never rise until my tears and prayers
    Have won his Grace to come in person hither,
    And take perforce my husband from the abbess.

*2.M.*By this I think the dial points at five :
    Anon I'm sure the Duke himself in person
    Comes this way to the melancholy vale ;   120
    The place of death and sorry execution,
    Behind the ditches of the abbey here.

Ang. Upon what cause ?

2.M. To see a reverend Syracusian merchant,
　　　Who put unluckily into this bay
　　　Against the laws and statutes of this town,
　　　Beheaded publicly for his offence.

Ang. See where they come, we will behold his death.

Luc. Kneel to the Duke before he pass the abbey.

　　　Enter Duke, attended ; Ægeon bareheaded ; with the
　　　　　Headsman and other Officers

Du. Yet once again proclaim it publicly,　　　　　130
　　　If any friend will pay the sum for him,
　　　He shall not die ; so much we tender him.

Adr. Justice, most sacred Duke, against the abbess !

Du. She is a virtuous and a reverend lady,
　　　It cannot be that she hath done thee wrong.

Adr. May it please your Grace, Antipholus my husband,—
　　　Whom I made lord of me, and all I had,
　　　At your important letters,—this ill day
　　　A most outrageous fit of madness took him ;
　　　That desperately he hurried through the street,—　　140
　　　With him his bondman, all as mad as he,—
　　　Doing displeasure to the citizens,
　　　By rushing in their houses, bearing thence
　　　Rings, jewels, any thing his rage did like.
　　　Once did I get him bound, and sent him home,

Whilst to take order for the wrongs I went,
That here and there his fury had committed ;
Anon, I wot not by what strong escape,
He broke from those that had the guard of him,
And with his mad attendant and himself,   150
Each one with ireful passion, with drawn swords,
Met us again, and, madly bent on us,
Chas'd us away ; till, raising of more aid,
We came again to bind them : then they fled
Into this abbey, whither we pursued them,
And here the abbess shuts the gates on us,
And will not suffer us to fetch him out,
Nor send him forth, that we may bear him hence.
Therefore, most gracious Duke, with thy command
Let him be brought forth, and borne hence for help. 160

Du. Long since thy husband serv'd me in my wars,
And I to thee engag'd a prince's word,
When thou didst make him master of thy bed,
To do him all the grace and good I could.
Go, some of you, knock at the abbey-gate,
And bid the lady abbess come to me.
I will determine this before I stir.

Enter a Servant

Ser. O mistress, mistress, shift and save yourself !
My master and his man are both broke loose,

Beaten the maids a-row, and bound the doctor,   170
Whose beard they have sing'd off with brands of fire,
And ever as it blaz'd, they threw on him
Great pails of puddled mire to quench the hair :
My master preaches patience to him, and the while
His master with scissors nicks him like a fool ;
And sure, unless you send some present help,
Between them they will kill the conjurer.

*Adr.*Peace, fool ! thy master and his man are here,
And that is false thou dost report to us.

Ser. Mistress, upon my life, I tell you true ;   180
I have not breath'd almost since I did see it.
He cries for you, and vows, if he can take you,
To scorch your face, and to disfigure you.   *Cry within*
Hark, hark ! I hear him, mistress : fly, be gone !

Du. Come, stand by me, fear nothing.   Guard with halberds !

*Adr.*Ay me, it is my husband !   Witness you,
That he is borne about invisible :
Even now we hous'd him in the abbey here ;
And now he 's there, past thought of human reason.
   Enter Antipholus of Ephesus and Dromio of Ephesus

*A.E.*Justice, most gracious Duke, O, grant me justice !   190
Even for the service that long since I did thee,
When I bestrid thee in the wars, and took
Deep scars to save thy life ; even for the blood

69

    That then I lost for thee, now grant me justice.

Æg. Unless the fear of death doth make me dote,
    I see my son Antipholus, and Dromio.

A.E. Justice, sweet prince, against that woman there !
    She whom thou gav'st to me to be my wife,
    That hath abused and dishonour'd me,
    Even in the strength and height of injury :   200
    Beyond imagination is the wrong
    That she this day hath shameless thrown on me.

Du. Discover how, and thou shalt find me just.

A.E. This day, great Duke, she shut the doors upon me,
    While she with harlots feasted in my house.

Du. A grievous fault ! Say, woman, didst thou so ?

Adr. No, my good lord : myself, he and my sister
    To-day did dine together. So befal my soul
    As this is false he burthens me withal !

Luc. Ne'er may I look on day, nor sleep on night,   210
    But she tells to your Highness simple truth !

Ang. O perjur'd woman ! They are both forsworn,
    In this the madman justly chargeth them.

A.E. My liege, I am advised what I say,
    Neither disturbed with the effect of wine,
    Nor heady-rash, provok'd with raging ire,
    Albeit my wrongs might make one wiser mad.
    This woman lock'd me out this day from dinner :

That goldsmith there, were he not pack'd with her,
Could witness it, for he was with me then ;   220
Who parted with me to go fetch a chain,
Promising to bring it to the Porpentine,
Where Balthazar and I did dine together.
Our dinner done, and he not coming thither,
I went to seek him : in the street I met him,
And in his company that gentleman.
There did this perjur'd goldsmith swear me down
That I this day of him receiv'd the chain,
Which, God he knows, I saw not : for the which
He did arrest me with an officer.   230
I did obey, and sent my peasant home
For certain ducats : he with none return'd.
Then fairly I bespoke the officer
To go in person with me to my house.
By the way we met my wife, her sister, and a rabble
          more
Of vile confederates.   Along with them
They brought one Pinch, a hungry lean-fac'd villain,
A mere anatomy, a mountebank,
A threadbare juggler, and a fortune-teller,
A needy, hollow-eyed, sharp-looking wretch,   240
A living dead man : this pernicious slave,
Forsooth, took on him as a conjurer ;

And, gazing in mine eyes, feeling my pulse,
And with no face, as 'twere, outfacing me,
Cries out, I was possess'd.   Then all together
They fell upon me, bound me, bore me thence,
And in a dark and dankish vault at home
There left me and my man, both bound together,
Till, gnawing with my teeth my bonds in sunder,
I gain'd my freedom ; and immediately 250
Ran hither to your Grace, whom I beseech
To give me ample satisfaction
For these deep shames, and great indignities.

Ang. My lord, in truth, thus far I witness with him,
That he din'd not at home, but was lock'd out.

Du. But had he such a chain of thee, or no ?

Ang. He had, my lord, and when he ran in here,
These people saw the chain about his neck.

2.M. Besides, I will be sworn these ears of mine
Heard you confess you had the chain of him, 260
After you first forswore it on the mart :
And thereupon I drew my sword on you ;
And then you fled into this abbey here,
From whence, I think, you are come by miracle.

A.E. I never came within these abbey-walls,
Nor ever didst thou draw thy sword on me :
I never saw the chain, so help me Heaven !

And this is false you burthen me withal.

Du. Why, what an intricate impeach is this !
　I think you all have drunk of Circe's cup. 270
　If here you hous'd him, here he would have been ;
　If he were mad, he would not plead so coldly :
　You say he din'd at home, the goldsmith here
　Denies that saying.　Sirrah, what say you ?

D.E. Sir, he din'd with her there, at the Porpentine.

Cou. He did, and from my finger snatch'd that ring.

A.E. 'Tis true, my liege, this ring I had of her.

Du. Saw'st thou him enter at the abbey here ?

Cou. As sure, my liege, as I do see your Grace.

Du. Why, this is strange.　Go call the abbess hither. 280
　I think you are all mated, or stark mad.

Exit one to the Abbess

Æg. Most mighty Duke, vouchsafe me speak a word :
　Haply I see a friend will save my life,
　And pay the sum that may deliver me.

Du. Speak freely, Syracusian, what thou wilt.

Æg. Is not your name, sir, call'd Antipholus ?
　And is not that your bondman, Dromio ?

D.E. Within this hour I was his bondman, sir,
　But he, I thank him, gnaw'd in two my cords :
　Now I am Dromio, and his man, unbound. 290

Æg. I am sure you both of you remember me.

*D.E.*Ourselves we do remember, sir, by you ;
  For lately we were bound, as you are now.
  You are not Pinch's patient, are you, sir ?

Æg. Why look you strange on me ? you know me well.

*A.E.*I never saw you in my life till now.

Æg. O, grief hath chang'd me since you saw me last,
  And careful hours with time's deformed hand
  Have written strange defeatures in my face :
  But tell me yet, dost thou not know my voice ? 300

*A.E.*Neither.

Æg. Dromio, nor thou ?

D.E.   No, trust me, sir, nor I.

Æg. I am sure thou dost.

*D.E.*Ay, sir, but I am sure I do not, and whatsoever a man
  denies, you are now bound to believe him.

Æg. Not know my voice !   O time's extremity,
  Hast thou so crack'd and splitted my poor tongue
  In seven short years, that here my only son
  Knows not my feeble key of untun'd cares ?
  Though now this grained face of mine be hid 310
  In sap-consuming winter's drizzled snow,
  And all the conduits of my blood froze up ;
  Yet hath my night of life some memory ;
  My wasting lamps some fading glimmer left ;
  My dull deaf ears a little use to hear :

All these old witnesses—I cannot err—
: Tell me thou art my son Antipholus.

*A.E.*I never saw my father in my life.

Æg. But seven years since, in Syracusa, boy,
Thou know'st we parted : but perhaps, my son,   320
Thou sham'st to acknowledge me in misery.

*A.E.*The Duke, and all that know me in the city,
Can witness with me that it is not so :
I ne'er saw Syracusa in my life.

Du. I tell thee, Syracusian, twenty years
Have I been patron to Antipholus,
During which time he ne'er saw Syracusa :
I see thy age and dangers make thee dote.

Re-enter Abbess, with Antipholus of Syracuse and
Dromio of Syracuse

*Abb.*Most mighty Duke, behold a man much wrong'd.

All gather to see them

*Adr.*I see two husbands, or mine eyes deceive me.   330

Du. One of these men is Genius to the other ;
And so of these, which is the natural man,
And which the spirit ? who deciphers them ?

D.S. I, sir, am Dromio : command him away.

*D.E.*I, sir, am Dromio ; pray, let me stay.

*A.S.*Ægeon art thou not ? or else his ghost ?

*D.S.*O, my old master ! who hath bound him here ?

Abb. Whoever bound him, I will loose his bonds,
And gain a husband by his liberty.
Speak, old Ægeon, if thou be'st the man   340
That hadst a wife once call'd Æmilia,
That bore thee at a burthen two fair sons :
O, if thou be'st the same Ægeon, speak,
And speak unto the same Æmilia !

Du. Why, here begins his morning story right :   †
These two Antipholuses, these two so like,
And these two Dromios, one in semblance,—
Besides her urging of her wreck at sea,—
These are the parents to these children,
Which accidentally are met together.   350

Æg. If I dream not, thou art Æmilia :
If thou art she, tell me, where is that son
That floated with thee on the fatal raft ?

Abb. By men of Epidamnum he and I
And the twin Dromio, all were taken up ;
But by and by rude fishermen of Corinth
By force took Dromio and my son from them,
And me they left with those of Epidamnum.
What then became of them I cannot tell ;
I to this fortune that you see me in.   360

Du. Antipholus, thou cam'st from Corinth first ?

A.S. No, sir, not I, I came from Syracuse.

76

Du. Stay, stand apart, I know not which is which.

A.E. I came from Corinth, my most gracious lord,—

D.E. And I with him.

A.E. Brought to this town by that most famous warrior,
    Duke Menaphon, your most renowned uncle.

Adr. Which of you two did dine with me to-day ?

A.S. I, gentle mistress.

Adr.   And are not you my husband ?

A.E. No, I say nay to that.   370

A.S. And so do I, yet did she call me so :
    And this fair gentlewoman, her sister here,
    Did call me brother.   *(to Luciana)* What I told you
        then,
    I hope I shall have leisure to make good ;
    If this be not a dream I see and hear.

Ang. That is the chain, sir, which you had of me.

A.S. I think it be, sir, I deny it not.

A.E. And you, sir, for this chain arrested me.

Ang. I think I did, sir, I deny it not.

Adr. I sent you money, sir, to be your bail,   380
    By Dromio, but I think he brought it not.

D.E. No, none by me.

A.S. This purse of ducats I receiv'd from you,
    And Dromio my man did bring them me.
    I see we still did meet each other's man,

77

And I was ta'en for him, and he for me,
And thereupon these errors are arose.

A.E. These ducats pawn I for my father here.

Du. It shall not need, thy father hath his life.

Cou. Sir, I must have that diamond from you. 390

A.E. There, take it, and much thanks for my good cheer.

Abb. Renowned Duke, vouchsafe to take the pains
To go with us into the abbey here,
And here at large discoursed all our fortunes,
And all that are assembled in this place,
That by this sympathized one day's error
Have suffer'd wrong : go, keep us company,
And we shall make full satisfaction.
Thirty-three years have I but gone in travail
Of you, my sons, and till this present hour 400
My heavy burthen ne'er delivered.
The Duke, my husband, and my children both,
And you the calendars of their nativity,
Go to a gossips' feast, and go with me ;
After so long grief, such nativity !

Du. With all my heart, I 'll gossip at this feast.

Exeunt all but A. S., A. E., D. S., and D. E.

D.S. Master, shall I fetch your stuff from ship-board ?

A.E. Dromio, what stuff of mine hast thou embark'd ?

D.S. Your goods that lay at host, sir, in the Centaur.

A.S. He speaks to me.   I am your master, Dromio :   410
  Come, go with us, we 'll look to that anon ;
  Embrace thy brother there, rejoice with him.
        Exeunt A. S. and A. E.

D.S. There is a fat friend at your master's house,
  That kitchen'd me for you to-day at dinner :
  She now shall be my sister, not my wife.

D.E. Methinks you are my glass, and not my brother ;
  I see by you I am a sweet-fac'd youth.
  Will you walk in to see their gossiping ?

D.S. Not I, sir, you are my elder.

D.E. That 's a question, how shall we try it ?   420

D.S. We 'll draw cuts for the senior, till then lead thou first.

D.E. Nay, then, thus :
  We came into the world like brother and brother ;
  And now let 's go hand in hand, not one before another.
        Exeunt

Notes

II. i. 111-13. The passage is given as in F, but is clearly corrupt beyond the reach of even probable amendment.

II. ii. 139. *crime*; perhaps we should read with Warburton *grime*; if so, an auditory, not a graphical, error.

II. ii. 144. *I live distain'd*; this will not do as it stands, since *distain'd* in Shakespeare means *stained*, not *unstained*. The emendation *unstain'd* is easy from the point of view of sense, but hopeless either graphically or auditorily. The New Cambridge editors transpose the two lines of the couplet, but this seems to split the couplet awkwardly, and to leave *undishonoured* as out of keeping in its new context as *distain'd* was before.

II. ii. 205. *above*; no doubt this suits the use of the upper stage in the next scene, but I suspect that we should read *alone*.

III. i. 48. I accept the New Cambridge editors' arrangement, whereby Dromio is ' within ' unseen, but the two women appear ' above.'

III. ii. 2, 4. It seems that we must either read with Theobald *Antipholus, hate*, retaining the F *ruinate*, or retain the F *Antipholus* and read with Capell *ruinous*. Neither is satisfactory; the one makes awkward metre, and the other changes a good Shakespearean word.

III. ii. 118. An allusion to the civil war between Henry IV and the League.

III. ii. 120. *chalky cliffs*; no doubt, as the New Cambridge editors are the first to point out, her teeth.

IV. i. 56. *by me*; F *me by*. The not difficult transposition seems to be simpler than the notes in which the meaning is usually expounded.

IV. ii. 28. *sweet, now*; this is not satisfactory. 'The rude clown,' as the New Cambridge editors remark, can hardly address the ladies as 'sweet.' But I am not clear that he could well tell them to *sweat*, as the same editors do.

IV. ii. 32. *Tartar limbo*; a complicated joke: *limbo* was commonly used (though inaccurately) for 'Hell,' but also (and more accurately) as a metaphor for 'prison.' *Tartar* was a common abbreviation for 'Tartarus' (Hell). But Dromio is implying that a 'Tartar' (in the ethnological sense) Hell-prison is worse than a Christian one.

IV. ii. 35. *fairy*; commonly emended to *fury*, which is probable but not essential, since a fairy could be malignant; *cf.* in *Hamlet*, *No fairy takes, nor witch hath power to charm.*

IV. ii. 46. *Mistress Redemption*; F 1 reads *Mistris redemption*, and editors have almost universally inserted a comma and read *send him, mistress, redemption.* . . . The 'New Cambridge' editors point out that Dromio's mind in this and the next scene seems to be full of the miracle and morality plays, and I am inclined to think that they are therefore right in accepting F 4's capitalisation of *Redemption*.

IV. iii. 13. *Adam*; *i.e.* the sergeant in his 'buff'-jerkin, either the 'coats of skins' or the quibble on 'buff,' *i.e.* naked.

IV. iii. 22-28. This is one of those vexatious passages, not uncommon when one of Shakespeare's clowns has taken the bit firmly in his teeth, that are wearisomely insignificant unless the points of the quibbles are grasped, but in which the points are to modern taste so blunt that the passage is scarcely less wearisome when they have been laboriously explained. Dromio is punning on three senses of *case*, 'affair,' the leather case containing the base-viol, and the suit of buff leather of the prison officer; possibly on *tired* and 'attired'; certainly on two senses of *durance*, 'imprisonment' and 'a stout kind of cloth' (or possibly taken as being the same as buff; *cf.*

Henry IV, ' Is not a buff jerkin a most sweet robe of durance ? ') ; and on four senses of *rest*, ' respite,' ' arrest,' ' the rest for a pike ' and ' to set up one's rest ' meaning ' to risk all.'

IV. iii. 60. *Master, if you do . . .*; F omits the *you*, which seems necessary for any sense, but even so the sense is not much to boast of. *Spoon-meat* means ' food for infants ' and so ' delicacies.' F has no comma between *do* and *expect*, and the simplest emendation that would give point, if one could find a graphical explanation of it, would be to omit *or*. *I.e.* ' the kind of spoon-meat you may expect here is the kind that must be eaten with a *long* spoon.'

V. i. 270. *Circe's cup* ; Circe gave the followers of Odysseus a draught which turned them into beasts.

V. i. 345. It looks as though some lines must have been omitted in which the Abbess did mention a wreck at sea. (It is perhaps worth noticing that she does use the phrase in V. i. 49, though the Duke does not hear her.) Matters are not improved by the transference of the lines to follow the Abbess's next speech, since there is no mention of the wreck in that either.

Glossary

MANY words and phrases in Shakespeare require glossing, not because they are in themselves unfamiliar, but for the opposite reason, that Shakespeare uses in their Elizabethan and unfamiliar sense a large number of words which seem so familiar that there is no incentive to look for them in the glossary. It is hoped that a glossary arranged as below will make it easy to see at a glance what words and phrases in any particular scene require elucidation. A number of phrases are glossed by what seems to be, in their context, the modern equivalent rather than by lexicographical glosses on the words which compose them.

Act First

SCENE I

line

8 GUILDER, a Dutch coin (*in plural, loosely*, money)

22 QUIT, cancel

41 FACTOR, agent

64 INSTANCE, hint

73 FOR FASHION, to be in the fashion

line

77 SINKING-RIPE, on the point of sinking

95 THAT, what

99 WORTHILY, justly

158 LIFELESS END, the end that is death.

SCENE II

9 HOST, put up

18 MEAN, chance

41 ALMANAC OF MY TRUE DATE, *i.e.* my twin

44 CAPON, chicken

52 PENITENT, undergoing penance (*i.e.* fasting).

53 STOP IN YOUR WIND, 'shut up'

64 POST, the post on which a tavern reckoning was scored

80 STAND ON TRICKS, play the buffoon

96 O'ER-RAUGHT, cheated

97 COZENAGE, trickery

102 LIBERTIES, license

Act Second

SCENE I

line

15 LASH'D, fastened
17 HIS, its
25 ATTEND ON THEIR ACCORDS, study to secure their complaisance
56 HORN-MAD, mad like a bull (*with a play on the horns as an emblem of cuckoldry*)
87 MINIONS, darlings.

line

94 BAIT, allure
98 FAIR, beauty
100 PALE, fence
101 STALE, dupe.
103 DISPENSE WITH, condone
110 HIS, its
116 FOND, silly

SCENE II

29 MAKE A COMMON OF, intrude on
34 SCONCE, *here* head; *three lines lower* screen
72 FINE AND RECOVERY, *a legal quibble* (cf. *Hamlet*, V. i. 112)

76 EXCREMENT, outgrowth
92 FALSING, false
95 TIRING, attiring
179 SHE MOVES ME FOR HER THEME, I am her text

Act Third

SCENE I

4 CARCANET, necklace
18 SAD, sober
32 MOME, dolt
    MALT-HORSE, a heavy kind of horse
    PATCH, fool
42 OWE, own
45, MICKLE, much
48 COIL, ado

51 SET IN MY STAFF, make myself at home?
80 CROW, crowbar
99 IN THE STIRRING PASSAGE, when everyone is up and about
100 A VULGAR COMMENT WILL BE MADE OF IT, it will be the talk of the town
116 PORPENTINE, Porcupine

SCENE II

line		line	
22	CREDIT, credulity	129	CARRACK, trading-ship
36	FOLDED, concealed	132	DIVINER, detector
58	WINK, close the eyes	139	CURTAL, docked
86	SIR-REVERENCE, *a corruption of*	140	TURN I' THE WHEEL, serve as
	Saving your reverence		turn-spit
97	SWART, black	172	YOU ARE A MERRY MAN, 'You
117	REVERTED, revolted		will have your joke'

Act Fourth

SCENE II

22	STIGMATICAL, branded	37	BACK-FRIEND, false friend
	MAKING, physical make-up	39	DRY-FOOT, on a weak scent (*of*
33	EVERLASTING, the characteristic		*the foot only*)
	material for the uniform of	49	BAND, promise
	constables	65	CONCEIT, apprehension

SCENE III

24	SOB, a rest given to a tired horse	39	ANGELS, *pun on* coins
38	HOY, coasting vessel	47	AVOID, avaunt

SCENE IV

6	ATTACH'D, arrested	91	DEADLY, death-like
45	CONJURER, exorcist	112	PEEVISH, obstinate
49	ECSTASY, madness	141	AT LARGE, in full

THE COMEDY OF ERRORS

Act Fifth

SCENE I